RAPHAEL'S MISSION

in the Light of the Science of the Spirit

Rudolf Steiner

From Rudolf Steiner: *Ergebnisse der Geistesforschung*.
(Some Results of Spiritual Research).
GA 62. Lecture IX, 30th January 1913 in Berlin.

Translated by Peter Stebbing

Cover designed by Peter Stebbing

Cover drawing:
Raphael: Cartoon for St. George
ca. 1504–05, Uffizi Gallery, Florence
Pen and brown ink, 26.5 x 26.7 cm

The "R" Initial graphic was designed by Rudolf Steiner

Rudolf Steiner Archive & e.Lib
Visit the website at https://www.rsarchive.org/

Printed in the United States of America

First Printing: August 2018
The e.Lib, Inc.

ISBN-13: 978-1-948302-02-9
ISBN-10: 1-948302-02-0

All the world will want to know about the life-work of such a human being, for Raphael has become one of the pillars upon which the higher culture of the human spirit is founded.

Herman Grimm

RAPHAEL'S MISSION

in the Light of the Science of the Spirit

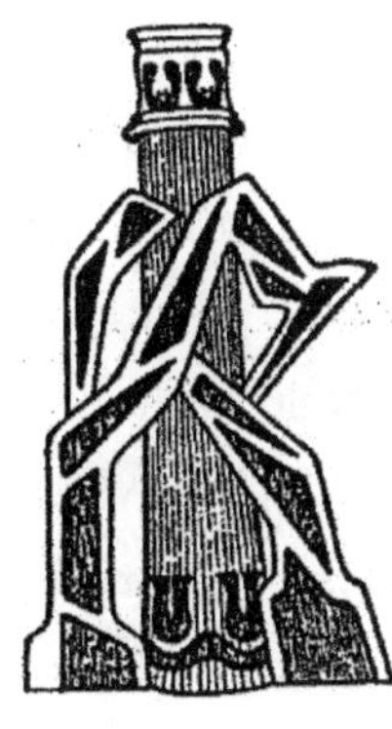

aphael belongs to those figures in mankind's spiritual history that appear all at once, like a star, who are simply there, so that one has the feeling, they arise quite suddenly from indeterminate substrata of humanity's spiritual development — disappearing again after deeply impressing their being upon this spiritual history. Closer observation reveals that such individualities, of whom one had at first assumed, they light up like a star and disappear again, actually incorporate themselves into cultural life as a whole, as into a great organism. One has this feeling quite especially with Raphael.

Herman Grimm [1828-1901], the eminent art historian, of whom I was able to speak here last time, attempted to trace Raphael's influence, his renown, through the times that follow Raphael's own age, up to our own day. He was able to show that Raphael's creations worked on after his death like a living, unified stream of spiritual development that continues beyond his death, reaching to the present. If Herman Grimm was able to show this, one would like to say on the other hand: The preceding age leaves us with the impression that it already points in a certain respect to Raphael's later entry into world evolution, just as a limb is an integral part of an organism.

In calling to mind a saying of Goethe's, one would like to transpose it, as it were, from the realm of space to the realm of time. Goethe once made the following significant utterance: "How can the human being relate himself to the infinite, other than by gathering together all his spiritual forces, drawn from many directions, asking himself: Is it permissible to think of yourself as the centre of this eternally existing universal order, when it leads at the same time to a persistent circling around an absolute mid-point?" [From: *Wilhelm Meisters Wanderjahre*, Vol. 1, Chapter 10.]

In applying this saying to temporal evolution, one would like to add: in a certain respect the gods of Homer, described by him in such a grandiose manner almost a thousand years before the founding of Christianity, would lose something for us, in looking back into pre-historic times, if we were not able to see them as they re-emerged in the soul of Raphael. Only there do they attain a certain completion in the powerful visual expression of Raphael's creations. Thus, what Homer brought forth long before the advent of Christianity joins itself for us to an organic whole through what arose from Raphael's soul in the sixteenth century.

And, by the same token, if we direct our gaze to the biblical figures of which the New Testament tells us and then contemplate the works of Raphael, we have the sense that something would at once be lacking for us if the creative power in Raphael's Madonnas and similar pictures, arising from biblical tradition and legends, had not been added to the descriptions of the Bible. One would like to say, Raphael not only lives on in the centuries that follow him; what preceded him joins with his own creative activity to form an organic whole — even if this becomes evident only from a later historical viewpoint.

Thus, an expression that Lessing [Gotthold Ephraim, 1729-1781] made use of in an important connection, in referring to "the education of the human race," appears in a special light. We see how a uniform spiritual element flows through humanity's development and how this shines forth quite especially in such outstanding figures as Raphael. What we have often been able to emphasize from a spiritual scientific standpoint in regard to the development of humanity — concerning the repeated earth-lives of the human being — takes on further significance in contemplating what has been said. We become aware of the significance of the fact that the human spirit appears again and again in repeated earth-lives throughout the various epochs of humanity, bearing from one age to another what is to be implanted in mankind's spiritual development. Spiritual science seeks meaning and significance in human evolution. It does not want merely to present what happens sequentially in an ongoing straight line of development, but rather to assign an overall meaning to single periods. In appearing again and again in earth-lives that follow each other, the human soul comes onto this earth so as to be able to experience something new each time. Thus, we can really speak of an education the human soul undergoes in passing through various earth-lives; an education by means of all that is cultivated and achieved by the common spirit of humanity.

What is put forward here from a spiritual scientific standpoint concerning Raphael's relation to the general development of humanity over the last centuries is not meant as a philosophical, historical construct. It arises rather as a natural outcome of considering Raphael's creative activity from all manner of viewpoints. These reflections are not the result of an urge to elaborate on humanity's spiritual life philosophically. What is said has arisen for me after contemplating Raphael's creations from many points of view — crystallizing quite naturally into what I wish to present. However, it will not be possible to enter into particular works of Raphael as such, since this would require showing such works at the same time. But the total works of Raphael also coalesce in feeling to an overall impression. Having studied Raphael, one bears something of a total impression in one's soul. And then one may ask: How does it stand with this overall impression as regards the development of humanity?

Our attention is necessarily drawn to an important age with which Raphael is intimately connected, the age that coincides with the development of the ancient Greek culture. What the Greeks attained and what they experienced out of their inherent nature presents itself as a kind of middle epoch in the development of humanity. What precedes Greek culture, which is concurrent in a certain respect with the founding of Christianity, presents a quite different aspect from what follows it. If we consider the human being in the time prior to Greek culture, we find that the soul and spirit were much more intimately connected with the external bodily nature than was the case in subsequent periods. What we may call the "internalizing" of the human soul, the withdrawal of the human soul in turning to the spirit, in wanting to contemplate what underlies the spiritual in the world — this did not exist in the same measure as it does today for the times preceding the Greek period. For human beings of that earlier time it was rather that in making use of their bodily organs, the spiritual secrets of existence illuminated their souls simultaneously. A detached view of the sense world, such as we find in today's conventional science, did not exist in those older times. The human being beheld objects with his senses, sensing at the same time, in having the impression before him, what lives and weaves in things of a soul-spiritual nature. The spiritual resulted for human beings from the things themselves, from making use of their sense organs. A withdrawal from sense impressions, in giving oneself over to inner experience, so as to arrive at the spiritual in the world, was not necessary in older times.

If we go very far back in the development of humanity, we find that what may be called, in the best sense of the word, "clairvoyant contemplation of things," was a general property of the humanity of primeval times. This clairvoyant contemplation was not attained in separate states but was simply there and as natural as sense perception. Then came Greek civilization with its own characteristic world of which it can be said that, though the internalizing of spiritual life begins here, what the spirit experiences inwardly is still seen in connection with what goes on externally in the sense world. In Greece the sensory and the psycho-spiritual hold each other in balance. The spiritual was no longer given in such an immediate fashion together with sense perception as in the time preceding Greece. The spiritual welled up as it were in the Greek soul as something inwardly separate, but as something felt in directing the senses out into the world. The human being became aware of the spiritual, not *in* the things of the external world, but in connection with them. In the time preceding Greece, the human soul was poured, as it were, into the bodily nature. It had freed itself from the bodily nature to some extent in Greece, but the soul-spiritual held the bodily nature in balance throughout the time of ancient Greece. For that reason, the creations of the Greeks appear as fully permeated with spirituality as what presented itself to their senses. — Then came the times that followed Greece, times in which the human spirit internalizes — in which it was no longer granted it to receive the spiritual element that lives and weaves in things along with sense impressions. These are times in which the human soul had to withdraw into itself and experience its own forces through conscious effort, in advancing to the spiritual. The human soul had to experience spiritual contemplation of things and sensory observation as, so to speak, two worlds.

What has just been said becomes fully evident in considering a spirit such as St. Augustine [A.D. 354-430], who is barely separated farther in time from the advent of Christianity than we are from the Reformation. Humanity's progress becomes apparent in comparing what St. Augustine experienced and set forth in his writings, with what has come down to us from the Greek world. What St. Augustine expounds in his *Confessions,* what he shows us of the soul battles in turning inward, what he reveals of an inner being altogether withdrawn from the external world — how impossible does this seem with regard to the spirits of ancient Greece! There we see everywhere how what lives in the soul unites with what happens in the external world.

The historical development of humanity shows itself divided as though by a mighty incision. On the one hand we have the culture of ancient Greece in which humanity holds the balance with respect to the soul-spiritual and the external physical. On the other hand, we have the founding of Christianity, that proceeds from everything the human being experiences inwardly, by means of inner battles and conscious effort — turning not to the outer world in sensing the riddles of existence, but to what the spirit can ascertain when giving itself over to purely soul-spiritual forces. Altogether different are those beautiful, those majestic and so perfect Greek gods, Zeus and Apollo, as though separated by a deep chasm from the Crucified One, from inner depth and power, undistinguished by external beauty. This is already the outer symbol for the profound turning point represented by Christianity and the culture of ancient Greece in the development of humanity. We see this turning point in the spirits that follow the Greek period, taking effect as an ever greater internalizing of the soul.

The inner deepening that took place in this way is characteristic of the further development of humanity. — If one would comprehend the development of humanity, one has to become clear in one's mind that we are living in an age which implies a progressive internalization in the sense of what has been said — whether we view it in terms of the immediate past, or in looking to the future. Thus, we can foresee a time in which a still greater chasm will loom between everything that goes on in the external world, what happens in the more or less mechanical life of the outer world, and what the human soul aspires to in wanting to ascend to an understanding of spiritual heights — in attempting to take the inner steps that lead to the spiritual. We are advancing more and more toward an age of further internalization. A significant turning point in regard to this progress of humanity toward inwardness since ancient Greek times is what has come down to us in Raphael's creations.

As a quite unusual spirit, Raphael places himself as though at a watershed of mankind's development. What precedes him is in a quite special sense the beginning of the turn toward inwardness. And what follows him presents a new chapter in this internalization of the human soul. Some of what I have to say in today's presentation may sound like a kind of symbolic reflection. But it should not be taken as a mere symbolic mode of expression. On account of Raphael's towering greatness, the attempt here is to grasp what can otherwise only be clothed in trivial concepts, as far as possible in broader concepts and ideas.

Attempting a glance into Raphael's inner being, it strikes us above all how, in the year 1483, this soul appears as a veritable "spring-time birth," undergoing an inner development and evolving brilliant creations. And when Raphael subsequently dies at thirty-seven, he is still young. So as to immerse ourselves in Raphael, in following the various stages of his development, let us turn our attention for the moment from historical events to Raphael's inner nature.

Herman Grimm has pointed out certain regular intervals in Raphael's development. Indeed, spiritual science has no need to be ashamed, in the face of disbelieving humanity, in pointing to certain cyclical laws, laws of a regular spiritual path, also of individuals, since a thinker of the calibre of Herman Grimm — without spiritual science — was led to recognize a regular cyclical development in Raphael. Herman Grimm refers to a work of Raphael that especially delights us in Milan, the "Marriage of the Virgin," [1504], as a completely new phenomenon in the whole of art history, that cannot be set alongside any previous work. Thus, out of indeterminate depths, Raphael brought forth something that distinguishes itself as being entirely new in spiritual evolution.

Noting in this way what, from birth on, was a predisposition in Raphael, taking account of his progression, we can sense with Herman Grimm how he enters upon certain four-year periods. It is remarkable how Raphael advances in cycles of four years. And if we contemplate such a four-year period, we see Raphael at a higher level each time. About four years after the "Marriage of the Virgin," he painted "The Entombment," four years later the frescoes of the "Camera della Segnatura," and so on, in stages of four years, until the work that stood unfinished next to his deathbed, the "Transfiguration of Christ" [1516-20].

Since everything in regard to Raphael's nature proceeds so harmoniously, we feel the need to consider it purely for itself. One then gains the impression that in the age of Raphael a quality of inwardness had to arise, quite especially in regard to the art of painting — an inwardness that had to realize itself in figures such as Raphael alone was able to bring about, born of profound soul experiences, though manifesting in sensory images. And does this not then in fact become part of history itself?

Having thus considered Raphael's inner nature, let us turn to the times and the surroundings into which he was placed. There we find that, while still a child growing up in Urbino, Raphael found himself in an environment that could have a stimulating and awakening effect on his decisive talents. A palace building had arisen in Urbino that aroused excitement throughout Italy. It could be said to have contributed to Raphael's initial harmonious disposition. However, we then see him transplanted to Perugia, to Florence and then to Rome. Basically, Raphael's life unfolded within a narrow circle. In viewing his life, how close in proximity do these places lie for us today. Raphael's entire world was circumscribed within a relatively narrow region, so far as the sense world was concerned. Only in spirit did he raise himself to other spheres.

In Perugia, where Raphael underwent his youthful development, bloody battles were the order of the day. The city was populated by a passionately aroused citizenry; noble families that lived in strife and discord, waged war on each other. One faction drove the other from the city. After a brief expulsion, the others attempted to seize the city again. And not a few times, the streets of Perugia were covered in blood and strewn with corpses. A history writer [Astorre Baglione.

See: Francesco Matarazzo: *Cronache della Città di Perugia.*] describes a peculiar scene, as do other reports of that time that are indeed quite odd. In lively fashion, we see a member of the city's nobility emerge, who, to avenge his relatives, storms into the city as a warrior. The writer describes how he rides on horseback through the streets, the embodiment of the spirit of war, massacring all in his way. But the description is such that the writer clearly had the impression: it is a matter of a justified vengeance being taken by the nobleman. The image in the historian's mind is of a warrior subjugating the enemy beneath his feet. In one of Raphael's pictures, the "St. George," we can sense this image the chronicler indicates. We have the immediate impression, it could not be otherwise than that Raphael let this scene work on him. What must appear outwardly so frightful for us, resurrects inwardly in Raphael's soul and becomes the starting point for one of the greatest and most significant pictures in the development of humanity.

Thus, Raphael witnessed a quarrelling, battling population around him. Confusion and chaos, war and strife reigned all around him in the city in which he pursued his apprenticeship with his first teacher, *Pietro Perugino*. We have the impression that two distinct worlds coexisted in the city: The one in which cruel and horrible things occurred, and another that lived inwardly in Raphael, having little to do with what went on around him.

Then in the year 1504 we again see Raphael transplanted, now to Florence. How did matters stand with Florence when

Raphael entered the city? First of all, by their conduct the inhabitants made the impression of being tired people, having undergone inner and outer states of agitation, of satiation and fatigue. — What all had not befallen Florence! Internal battles as in Perugia, bloody vendettas among patrician families, as well as battles with outside forces. But, roiling every soul in the city, there had also been the incisive experience of *Savonarola* [Girolamo Savonarola (1452-1498), prior of the Monastery of San Marco, burned at the stake at the instigation of Pope Alexander VI.] who had died a martyr's death not long before Raphael arrived in the city. We have the strange figure of Savonarola of the fiery tongue, lashing out against the deplorable state of affairs, the acts of cruelty on the part of the Church, against secularization, against the paganism of the Church. The stormy words of Savonarola reverberate in us if we give ourselves over to them; words with which he captivated all of Florence, so that people not only hung on every word, but worshipped him as though a higher spirit stood before them in that ascetic body.

As a kind of religious reformer Savonarola had transformed the city of Florence. His preachings pervaded not only religious ideas, but the entire city-state. Florence stood wholly under the influence of Savonarola, as though a divine republic of some sort were to be founded. And we then see Savonarola fall prey to the powers he had spoken out against, morally and religiously. The moving scene arises of Savonarola being led with his companions to the martyr's pyre. From the gallows he turned to look down upon the people gathered there, who had for so long been enthralled by him, having once hung on his every word. This was in May of the year 1498. Having now forsaken him, they viewed him as a heretic. However, in a few among them, including artists, the words of Savonarola still echoed on. After Savonarola had suffered a martyr's death, a painter of that time assumed the monk's habit, so as to continue working in his spirit, in his order. [Fra Bartolomeo, who became a Dominican in 1500.]

It is not difficult to imagine the tired atmosphere that lay over Florence. We see Raphael transposed into this atmosphere in the year 1504 — bringing, with his creative activity, the spirit's "breath of spring" that introduced into the city a spiritual fire, so to speak, though of a quite different kind from what Savonarola had been capable of. Taking account of the contrast between the mood of this city and Raphael's soul in its isolation (joining other artists and painters working in solitary workshops or elsewhere in Florence) a picture emerges that once again shows how Raphael stood inwardly apart from the external circumstances in which he found himself. We see the Roman popes, Alexander VI, Julius II, Leo X and the whole papal system that Savonarola had railed against and the reformers had opposed. But it transpires that in this papal system we have at the same time Raphael's patrons. We see Raphael in the service of this papacy. Inwardly, his soul has in truth little in common with what meets us, for example, in his patron

Julius II. The latter admitted to appearing to people as someone who "had the devil within him," and generally had the impulse to bare his teeth in confronting his enemies.

Nominally great figures, these popes were certainly not what Savonarola or his like-minded comrades would have called Christians. The papacy had passed over into heathenism, not in the old, but in a new sense. There was not much trace of Christian piety in these circles, though certainly of the desire for splendour and lust for power. Raphael becomes the servant of this heathenized Christendom. But such that something is created out of his soul by which the Christian ideas appear in many respects in a new form. We see the most heartfelt, the most delightful content of the world of Christian legends arise in the Madonna pictures and other works of Raphael. What a stark contrast there is between the inwardness of soul in Raphael's works and all that went on around him in Rome, when he became the outer servant of the popes. How was all this possible? Already, with his apprenticeship in Perugia, and then his time in Florence, we see how disparate were the actual circumstances and Raphael's inner nature. This was quite especially the case in Rome, where he created pictures of worldwide renown. Yet Raphael and his surroundings have to be taken into account if we are to acquire a proper idea of what lived within him.

Let us allow the pictures of Raphael to work upon us. For the moment, this cannot be done with individual pictures, though one of his best-known paintings may be singled out, so as to come to an understanding of the characteristic soul quality in Raphael. It is the "Sistine Madonna" in nearby Dresden, which almost everyone knows from the numerous reproductions found throughout the world. This shows itself to be one of the noblest, most magnificent works of art in the history of mankind. We see the Mother and Child float toward us over the clouds that cover the globe — out of an indeterminate realm of the spiritual-supersensible — enveloped and surrounded by clouds that seem naturally to take on human form. One of them as though condenses to become the Child of the Madonna. She calls forth a quite particular feeling in us. In permeating us inwardly, this enables us to forget all legendary ideas from which the image of the Madonna derives, as well as all Christian traditions that tell of the Madonna.

I should like to characterize, not in a dull manner, but as large-heartedly as possible what we are able to feel in regard to the Madonna. In considering human evolution in the sense of spiritual science we transcend the materialistic view. According to the natural scientific view, the lower creatures evolved first, ascending as far as the human being. However, from the standpoint of spiritual science we have to see the human being as having an existence over and above the lower kingdoms of nature. With the human being we have, in spiritual scientific terms, what is much older than all the creatures that stand in relative proximity to him in the kingdoms of nature.

For spiritual science the human being existed before the animal, the plant or even the mineral kingdom came into being. We look back into far distant perspectives of time in which what is now our innermost nature was already there, only later to unite itself with the kingdoms that stand below the human being. Thus, we see the essential being of Man descend, that in truth can only be comprehended in raising ourselves to the supersensible, to what is pre-earthly. By means of spiritual science we come to recognize that no adequate conception of the human being is to be gained from forces connected only with the earth. We must raise ourselves to super-terrestrial regions to see the approach of the human being. To speak metaphorically, we must feel how something floats toward the earthly — in turning our gaze, for instance, to the sunrise in a region such as that in which Raphael lived, to the gold-gleaming sunrise. There, even in natural existence, we can come to feel how something must be added to what is earthly, of forces that we can connect with the sun. Then there arises for us, out of the golden lustre, the symbol of what floats down in order to take on the vesture of the earthly.

In Perugia quite especially, one can have the sense that the eye beholds the same sunrise seen by Raphael and that the natural phenomenon of the rising sun grants us a feeling of what is celestial in the human being. Out of the clouds shone through by the sun-gold there can arise for us — or it can at least appear so — the image of the Madonna and Child as a symbol of the eternally celestial in the human being, that wafts down to the earth out of the extra-terrestrial. And below, separated by clouds, we have everything that only proceeds from the earthly. Our feeling-perception can rise to the most exalted spiritual heights, if — not theoretically and not abstractly but with our whole soul — we abandon ourselves to what affects us in Raphael's Madonna. It is a quite natural feeling one can have in regard to the world-famous picture in Dresden. And I should like to provide an example showing how it has had such an effect on some people, in quoting words written by Goethe's friend, *Karl August*, Duke of Weimar, concerning the "Sistine Madonna," following a visit to Dresden:

> With the Raphael adorning the collection there, it was for me as when, having climbed the heights of the Gotthard all day and traversed the Urseler Loch, one all of a sudden looks down on the blossoming, green valley below. As often as I saw it and looked away again, it always appeared only like an apparition. To me, even the most beautiful *Corregios* were only human pictures; in memory, their beautiful forms palpable to the senses. — Raphael, however, remained always like a mere breath, like one of those appearances the gods send us in female form, in our happiness or sorrow; like pictures that present themselves to us again in sleep, upon awakening or in dreaming, and having once seen, appear to us day and night ever afterwards, moving us in our inmost soul.

[Karl August to his friend Knebel, 14th October, 1783.]

And it is remarkable, what is to be found in following up the literature of those able to express something of a profound nature in viewing the "Sistine Madonna," as also other Raphael pictures. Again and again we find comparisons with light, with the sun, with what is luminous and what is spring-like in nature.

This affords us a glimpse into Raphael's soul. We see how, despite the conditions that prevailed around him, he holds converse with the eternal secrets of human development. We sense that, in his uniqueness, Raphael does not grow out of his surroundings, but points to a tremendous past. One does not then need to speculate. Such a soul looks out into the world's circumference and does not express the secrets of existence in ideas, but forms them into a picture. By virtue of its inner completeness such a soul is self-evidently mature in the highest degree and truly bears special forces of humanity in its whole disposition, — one that must have gone through epochs that poured tremendous things into the soul, so as to reappear in what we call the life of Raphael. How, we may ask, does this re-emerge?

We see the living content of Christian legends, of Christian traditions, arise in Raphael's pictures at a time in which Christianity had become pagan and given over to external pomp and outer splendour. Greek paganism was represented in its gods and venerated by the Greeks in their intoxication with beauty. We see Raphael giving form to the figures of Christian tradition in an age in which Greek treasures that had been buried for centuries under rubble and debris on Roman soil were being dug up again. We see Raphael among those excavating. Indeed, this Rome into which Raphael was transposed makes a remarkable impression.

What precedes this time? We see, first of all, the centuries in which Rome emerges, built on the egoism of individuals whose aim is to found a community in the external world based on what the human being signifies as the citizen of a state. When Rome had attained a certain height with the time of the Caesars, we see it absorb the Greek element into its spiritual life. We see Rome, though it had overwhelmed Greece politically, now overcome by Greece spirituality. Thus, the Greek element lived on in Rome. Greek art, to the extent it was absorbed by Rome lives on in what is Roman. Rome becomes permeated through and through by the Greek element.

But why does this Greek element not remain a characteristic feature of Italy's development over the following centuries? Why did something altogether different in fact make its appearance? Because, not long after this Greek element had poured itself into the Roman world, something else came, impressing its signature more strongly on what had developed on the soil of Italy: Christianity, the internalizing of Christianity. Something was now to speak to humanity, not as had the external sensory element of Greek cities, of Greek works of art, or Greek philosophy, but by addressing itself to the inner human being, taking hold of this human soul in inner battles. Hence, we see such figures arise as St. Augustine, personalities of a quite inward disposition.

But then, since all development runs its course cyclically, we again see a yearning for beauty arise, after human beings had undergone this internalizing and had lived for a long time without the same connection to external beauty. In the "outer" we once again see what is inward. In this regard, it is of significance when in Assisi the inwardly deepened life of *Francis of Assisi* appears in the works of *Giotto*, in which Christianity is able to speak directly to the human soul. — Even if we sense at the same time — the expression is permissible — something awkward and imperfect in Giotto's pictures, in bringing the inner nature of the human being to expression. We nonetheless have a direct line of ascent to the point where the most inward, the most impressive and noblest becomes manifest in outer form in Raphael and his contemporaries.

Entering in feeling into the way in which Raphael himself must have felt, we have to say to ourselves: In looking at a picture such as the "Madonna della Sedia," it strikes us, in contemplating the Madonna with the Child, along with the Child John, that we forget the rest of the world — forget above all that this Child held by the Madonna could be linked with what we know as the Golgotha experience. With Raphael's picture we forget everything that followed as the life of

Christ-Jesus. We give ourselves over entirely to the moment seen here. We have simply a Mother and Child, of which Herman Grimm said, it is the most exalted mystery to be met with in the outer world. We view the moment in serenity, as though nothing could connect onto it, either before or after. We are wholly taken up by the relationship of the Madonna and Child, separated from everything else. Thus, in always showing us the eternal in a given moment, Raphael's creations appear fundamentally complete in themselves.

What must a soul feel in creating in this manner? It cannot be seized inwardly by the burning fervour of Savonarola that feels the whole Christ tragedy within itself, in speaking its words of fury, or in addressing its hearers in uplifting, pious words. We cannot imagine that Raphael could have anything to do with Savonarola's spiritual orientation; or that so-called Christian fire could have held sway in Raphael. Nevertheless, we should not think that the Christian ideas could appear to us so vividly through Raphael — a human soul of such inwardness and completeness — if Christian fire had been altogether foreign to it.

One cannot create figures in an objective and well-rounded fashion if one is imbued with Savonarola's fire, borne along by the whole tragic mood of Christ, feeling oneself spurred on by this. A certain tranquillity and quite different Christian feelings must first have arisen in the soul. Even so, what has come to expression in Raphael's pictures could not have arisen if the very "nerve" of Christian inwardness had not lived in him. Is it not then reasonable to suppose: In the painter Raphael we have a soul that must already have brought that fire with it into physical existence that we perceive at work in Savonarola. If we see Raphael as bringing this fire along with him from earlier earth-lives, then we comprehend how he could be so inwardly serene, so inwardly complete, that this fire does not meet us as a consuming fire, destructive of enthusiasm, but as the tranquil element of creative activity. At this point I should like to say, one senses something in Raphael's natural abilities by means of which, in an earlier life, he could have spoken with the same fire as Savonarola. And it need not astonish us if Raphael's soul were to have re-arisen from a time in which Christianity was not yet present in the form of art, but received that mighty impulse at its immediate inception by which it became effective in the course of the centuries that followed.

Perhaps it is not too audacious, in attempting to understand Raphael, to put forward something like what has been said. For, whoever has learned, in immersing himself again and again in Raphael's works, to revere this individual in all its depths, to view it in its unfathomableness, is only able by means of such extended feelings to comprehend what speaks to us out of the miraculous works into which Raphael poured his soul.

Raphael's mission only appears to us in the right light when we seek, in the sense of Goethe's expression, "in a completed life" ["in einem abgelebten Leben"], the Christian fire that later manifests as serenity in Raphael. Then we come to understand why he had to place himself into the world in such an isolated manner. And we comprehend how the Raphael we have attempted to characterize — having experienced something "Savonarola-like" in an earlier life (only in an enhanced measure) — now became the Raphael we know from Renaissance Italy.

As already mentioned, in the time in which the Roman Empire drew near, in the Roman period of Greece, an internalizing of the soul had taken place. In the Renaissance, in Raphael's time, we see the ancient Greek culture, buried under rubble, reappearing. Rome was gradually filled with relics of Greece, with what had once beautified the city. The Roman population directed its attention once again to the forms the Greek spirit had created. In this period, we also see how the spirit of Plato, the spirit of Aristotle, the spirit of the Greek tragedians infuses Roman life. We see the Roman world conquered once again by Greek culture. For a spirit that had previously given itself over to the moral-religious view of Christianity, devoting itself in a prior life completely to such moral-religious impressions, Greek culture may be said to have had a renewing, fructifying effect, in appearing out of the rubble and ruins on the Italian peninsula.

Thus, if we see the moral-religious impulse of Christianity as integral to Raphael's innate faculties, what was not there in his disposition appeared in the Greek artefacts then being excavated before his eyes. The statues reappearing out of the rubble, products of the Greek spirit, the manuscripts that were recovered, had their effect on Raphael's soul as on no other. What united itself in this way as a result of his inner disposition — Christian feeling, combined with an especially spiritual devotion to what is cosmic — all this worked together with what was then re-emerging of the Greek spirit. These two things united in Raphael's soul, bringing it about that in his works we have what the time following Greece had generated — the inwardness with which Christianity had imbued the development of humanity — now finally brought to full expression in a world of forms, of pictures in which the purest Greek spirit speaks to us.

We see the remarkable phenomenon, that through Raphael the Greek element arises again within Christendom. In Raphael we see a Christianity appear in an age that, all around him, presents what is actually anti-Christian. In Raphael there lives a Christianity that goes far beyond the narrowness of the Christianity that had gone before, raising itself to a far-reaching conception of the world. However, this is a Christianity that does not merely point vaguely to infinite realms of the spiritual, but assumes artistic form — much as the ancient Greeks had united their idea of the gods with what lives and weaves formlessly in the universe, pressing this into figures that delight our senses.

In letting one or another of Raphael's creations work on us, in attempting to form an overall picture of his works in their exalted, perfect forms, they appear to us as possessing a wonderful excess of youth, for Raphael died at 37 years of age. Not for the sake of a grey theory, nor as a philosophical-historical "construct," but out of immediate feeling deriving from Raphael's works, it may be said: The lawful continuum of mankind's spiritual life presents itself to us most clearly with such a towering figure as Raphael.

Imagining the progress of spiritual life as a straight line in which cause and effect follow upon each other is truly not in accord with the facts. There is a saying that seems obvious, belonging to the "golden" pronouncements of humanity, namely, that life and nature make no leaps. However, in many respects life and nature make leaps all the time. We see this in the development of the plant, from the green leaf to the blossom, from the blossom to the fruit. There we see everything develop, yet we see that leaps are inevitable.

It is no different with the spiritual life of humanity, and this is connected with various evolutionary secrets. One of these is that a later epoch always has to reach back to an earlier one. Hence, just as the masculine and the feminine have to work together, so must the various Time Spirits work together, mutually fertilizing each other, so that further development can take place. Thus, the Roman period around the time of the Caesars had to be fertilized by the Greek element, for a new age to arise. And in the same way, the Time Spirit that then arose had to be fertilized by the Christian impulse, in order to make the internalizing possible that we see in St. Augustine and others. Similarly, more recently, such an inwardly advanced soul as Raphael had to be fertilized, made productive by the Greek element. Doubly buried though Greek culture then was, it yet reappeared, being doubly "extracted:" for the eyes in that the sculptures had been covered over by the soil of Italy; and for the souls, in the buried works of literature that revealed the Greek spirit. The centuries of the first Christian millennium, on the other hand, had been extraordinarily little touched by what lived in Greek philosophy, in Greek poetry.

Having been doubly buried, Greek culture waited, as it were, in a "beyond" for a later point in time when it could fertilize the human soul that had meanwhile been imbued with a new religion. Buried, withdrawn for outer eyes and buried likewise for souls that had no notion that it would develop further, it actually flowed on like a river that sometimes continues underground, out of sight, far below a mountain, returning afterwards to the surface. This Greek culture was buried outwardly for the senses, inwardly for the substrata of the soul. Now it reappeared. For spiritual sight it was excavated not only in that it was fetched from old manuscripts, but also in that people began to experience the world in the Greek manner once again, sensing how the spirit lives in everything material, how everything that is material is the revelation of the spiritual. People began to connect once more with what Plato and Aristotle had thought.

But Raphael was the individual on whom this could take effect most of all, since in his whole disposition he had fully assimilated the Christian impulses. With him this twice buried and twice resurrected Greek culture now brought it about that he was in a position to recreate the evolution of humanity in figures. How marvellously was he able to accomplish this in the pictures of the "Camera della Segnatura"! There we see the old spiritual contests arise again in pictures — the struggle of those spirits that had developed in the time of internalizing, that had not been there in the Greek period. That they could be viewed in this way in Raphael's time — for that, the whole period of internalizing was needed. We now see this internalizing painted on the walls of the papal rooms.

What the Greeks had conceived and formed into figures we now see internalized. The inner strivings and inner battles humanity had undergone we see infused with the Greek creative spirit, with the Greek artistic mood and sense for beauty, conjured onto the walls of the papal palace. The Greeks poured into their statues their conception of the way in which the gods worked upon the world. How human beings felt in approaching the secrets of existence presents itself to us in the picture often referred to as the "School of Athens." How the human soul had learned to view the Greek gods meets us in the remarkable recreation of the gods of Homer in the "Parnassus." These are not the gods of the

"*Iliad*" and the "*Odyssey*," but the gods as seen by a soul that had already gone through the epoch of internalization.

On the other wall we see the picture that must remain unforgettable to everyone, of whatever religious confession — as little as one can still gain an idea of it — the "*Disputa*," in which something most inward is depicted. The other picture presents what is attained by means of a certain philosophical striving, but in Greek beauty of form. In the picture opposite, the "Disputa," we encounter the most profound content the human being can experience. And the fact that we do not need to think in terms of a narrow Christian consciousness becomes evident here in that we find the Brahma, Vishnu and Shiva motifs expressed in a quite different way. We have before us what the human soul can experience inwardly of the Trinity — every soul, no matter what confession it belongs to. This appears to us not merely symbolically, in the symbolism of the Trinity in the upper part of the picture. It appears to us further in each countenance of the Church fathers and philosophers, in every motion of the hands, in the whole distribution of the figures, in the wonderful colour composition. It appears to us in the picture's totality. In the beautiful forms permeated with the Greek spirit we are presented with the human soul in its entire inwardness. The inwardness experienced in the course of one-and-a-half millennia arises once again, as outer revelation. In Raphael's pictures we see Christianity, not in the form of the paganism of the Roman popes and cardinals, but as the ancient Greek paganism, capable of creating beautiful, splendid figures.

Thus, Raphael stands at a turning point, at a watershed, pointing both to an earlier age that had preceded Christianity in the beauty of outer revelation, and to what may be seen as inherent in the "education of the human race," the internalizing of the human soul. Hence, in standing in front of these pictures of Raphael, these miraculous, unique works of art, they appear to us as the confluence of two ages clearly separate and distinct from each other: an age of outer experience and one of inner experience.

Yet, at the same time, in standing before these pictures, they open up a perspective into the future. For, with a feeling for what has been said, who does not sense that — in spite of all the externality that has still to evolve further in humanity's future — this internalizing must necessarily also progress further in the course of evolution? Indeed, the human soul will need to find periods of ever greater inwardness in subsequent lives.

If we turn to literature and study, not as an art scholar or mere reader, the works of a spirit such as Herman Grimm, who spared no effort in portraying the workings of human phantasy, we can understand the profound empathy with which he contemplated Raphael's creations. It becomes comprehensible, when, at a certain point in his work on Raphael we find words that take on special meaning. We see how he stood before Raphael's creations with heartfelt interest. One has to take account of what passed through Herman Grimm's soul at a certain point in his work on Raphael, in the first few pages where, in casting a glance at Raphael's emergence from ancient times, he only modestly touches on something. It is not evident, really, from where this thought comes. – In the middle of wider historical considerations into which Raphael is placed, a thought occurs to Herman Grimm and is written down: "I see before me developments of humanity, participation in which will be denied me, but that appear to me so radiantly beautiful that, on their account, it would be worth the trouble of beginning human life all over again." [In Herman Grimm: Das Leben Raphaels, (The Life of Raphael), p. 4.]

This yearning of Herman Grimm for "reincarnation" in the introduction to his Raphael book is remarkable and profoundly indicative of a particular feeling living in a human being who attempted to come to terms with Raphael and his connection to other epochs. Does one not sense what can be expressed more or less in saying: Works such as those of Raphael are not only an end-result. They lead us to acknowledge not only how grateful we have to be in regard to what past ages have given us. Such works call forth feelings in us such as the feeling of hope, since they strengthen us in our belief in the progress of humanity. We can say to ourselves, these works would not be as they are if humanity were not a unified being whose nature it is to advance. Thus, certainty and hope arise for us if we allow Raphael to work on us in the right way. And we can then say: Through what he created artistically, Raphael has spoken to humanity!

In contemplating the frescoes in the "Camera della Segnatura," we do of course sense the transience of the external work. From these works, frequently painted over, we can gain little idea of what Raphael once conjured onto the wall. We sense that at some point in the future human beings will no longer be able to experience the original works. But we know, humanity will progress ever further.

Fundamentally, the works of Raphael first embarked on their triumphal march when, with love and devotion, innumerable engravings, photographs and reproductions of his works were made. Their effect continues right into the reproductions. One can understand Herman Grimm when he relates that he once hung a large collotype [*Phototypie*] of the "Sistine Madonna" in his room and on entering, it was always as though he were not fully permitted to enter — as though the room now belonged to the picture as a sanctuary of the Madonna. Some will already have experienced how the soul actually becomes a different being than it otherwise is in ordinary life, when truly able to give itself over to a picture by Raphael — even a mere reproduction. Certainly, the originals will someday no longer exist. But, do the originals not still exist in other realms?

Herman Grimm frankly states in his book on Homer [See Herman Grimm: *Homers Ilias;* 2nd edition, Stuttgart and Berlin 1907, p. 473.]: We can also no longer fully enjoy the original works of Homer, since in ordinary life, without higher spiritual forces, we are no longer in a position to enter into all the nuances and expressions of the Greek language in their full beauty and power, in taking in Homer's "Iliad" and "Odyssey". There too we no longer have the originals. Even so, Homer's poetic works speak to us. But, what Raphael gave to humanity will live on as evidence of the fact that there was once a time in the development of humanity when, in the widest circles people were unable to immerse themselves in thoughts and written works, since that was far from being the norm at that time. However, in Raphael's creations the secrets of existence spoke to the eyes of human beings. The age of Raphael was one that read less, but that *looked* more. This makes it clear that that age was differently constituted. But what Raphael created will continue to have an effect in all future times. Confirmation of this will be what Raphael will continue to say to humanity. Thus, Raphael's creations will live on in the further course of human evolution, live on inwardly in lives that follow upon each other. In undergoing future lives, Raphael's spirit will have ever greater things, of an ever more inward nature, to impart to humanity.

Thus, spiritual science points to a further life in a two-fold sense; a living-on of a kind described in lectures that have been given and that will be spoken of further, becoming our guide in going through earthly existence in ever new epochs. It can be said to be entirely true, what Herman Grimm states in words summarizing what resulted for him from his overall study of Raphael: Even if Raphael's works will eventually have faded or been destroyed, Raphael will still live on. For, with him something has been implanted in the spirit of humanity that will forever germinate and bear fruit.

Every human soul sufficiently able to deepen itself in Raphael will come to feel this. Only in entering into a sense with which Herman Grimm was imbued — heightening and deepening this by means of spiritual science — do we come to understand Raphael fully. We indicated recently how close he stood, in contemplating Raphael ever and again, to spiritual science. — We can understand our relation to Raphael and such thoughts as have been ventured today can grow in us, if we conclude by summarizing what has been said in words of Herman Grimm:

> Human beings will always want to know about Raphael; about the beautiful young painter who surpassed all others; who was fated to die early. Whose death all Rome mourned. When the works of Raphael are finally lost, his name will remain engraved in human memory. [From Herman Grimm: *Das Leben Raphaels*, p. 1.]

Thus, did Herman Grimm express himself in beginning his discourse on Raphael. We understand these words; and we understand him again in concluding, at the end of his work on Raphael:

All the world will want to know about the life-work of such a human being, for Raphael has become one of the pillars upon which the higher culture of the human spirit is founded. We would fain draw nearer to him, since we have need of him for our well-being. [Ibid., p. 334.]

(*Translated by Peter Stebbing*)

Selected Bibliography

- Grimm Herman. *Das Leben Raphaels*. Cotta 1903/1927.
- Oberhuber, Konrad. *Raphael. The Paintings*. Prestel Verlag, Munich 1999.
- Steiner, Rudolf. *Art History as a Reflection of Inner Spiritual Impulses*. CW 292. Translated by Rory Bradley. SteinerBooks 2016.

On-line Resources

- On-line *Search* of Bn/GA# 62 texts
- Rudolf Steiner Archive & e.Lib. *The History of Art* part 1, Bn/GA# 292 translated by Christian van Arnim.
- Rudolf Steiner Archive & e.Lib. *The History of Art* part 2, Bn/GA# 292 translated by Hanna von Maltitz.
- Fine Art Presentations – e.Gallery. *Raphael* (Raffaello Sanzio)

About the translator

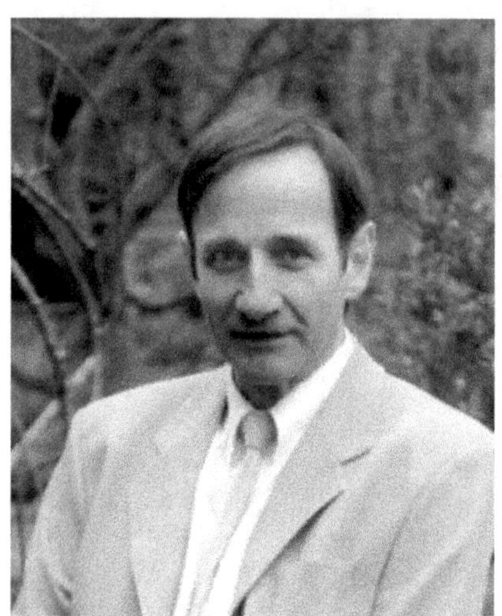

Born in Copenhagen, Denmark in 1941, Peter Stebbing attended Waldorf Schools in England. Having studied at art schools in Brighton and London, he emigrated to the United States in 1966, continuing his studies at Cornell University and earning the M.F.A. degree in painting in 1968.

While teaching design and colour courses over a period of six years in the City University of New York, he began a practical exploration of the scientific colour phenomena set forth by Goethe in his colour theory. This led eventually to a turning point – to the crucial question of finding a correspondingly lawful approach to colour in painting.

The new and wholly different training in colour experience begun in 1976 with the painter Gerard Wagner on the basis of Rudolf Steiner's motif sketches, resolved fundamental artistic questions with a coherent and systematic approach. Fully in accord with Goethe's discoveries and method, this approach may be termed "Goetheanistic."

Peter Stebbing subsequently established a painting school at the Threefold Educational Foundation in Spring Valley, N.Y., teaching there from 1983 until 1990. Since 1992 he has been director of the Arteum Painting School in Dornach, Switzerland. He is also the translator and editor of various anthroposophical art publications.

Other books by Peter Stebbing

- Margarita Woloschin, *The Green Snake. An Autobiography*. Floris Books, 2010. 431 pages paperback.
- Elisabeth Wagner-Koch and Gerard Wagner, *The Individuality of Colour. Contributions to a Methodical Schooling in Colour Experience*. 2nd edition. 128 pages. Hardcover. Rudolf Steiner Press, 2009.
- *The Goetheanum Cupola Motifs of Rudolf Steiner. Paintings by Gerard Wagner*. 236 pages. Hardcover. SteinerBooks, 2011.
- *Conversations about Painting with Rudolf Steiner. Recollections of Five Pioneers of the New Art Impulse*. 195 pages, 77 illustrations, hardcover. Steinerbooks, 2008.
- *Grimm's Fairy Tales. Paintings by Gerard Wagner*. 70 pages with 31 colour plates, hardcover. SteinerBooks, 2012.
- Rudolf Steiner, *The World of Fairy Tales*. 124 pages, paperback. SteinerBooks 2013.
- *The Art of Colour and the Human Form: Seven Motif Sketches of Rudolf Steiner: Studies by Gerard Wagner*. 218 pages, hardcover. Verlag des Ita Wegman Instituts, 2017.

www.ingramcontent.com/pod-product-compliance
Lightning Source LLC
LaVergne TN
LVHW010108110826
845155LV00028B/545

* 9 7 8 1 9 4 8 3 0 2 0 2 9 *